Aa

Bela Davis

Abdo
THE ALPHABET
Kids

abdopublishing.com

Published by Abdo Kids, a division of ABDO, PO Box 398166, Minneapolis, Minnesota 55439.
Copyright © 2017 by Abdo Consulting Group, Inc. International copyrights reserved in all countries.
No part of this book may be reproduced in any form without written permission from the publisher.

Printed in the United States of America, North Mankato, Minnesota.

102016
012017

THIS BOOK CONTAINS
RECYCLED MATERIALS

Photo Credits: iStock, Shutterstock

Production Contributors: Teddy Borth, Jennie Forsberg, Grace Hansen

Design Contributors: Christina Doffing, Candice Keimig, Dorothy Toth

Publisher's Cataloging in Publication Data

Names: Davis, Bela, author.

Title: Aa / by Bela Davis.

Description: Minneapolis, Minnesota : Abdo Kids, 2017 | Series: The alphabet |
    Includes bibliographical references and index.

Identifiers: LCCN 2016943880 | ISBN 9781680808773 (lib. bdg.) |
    ISBN 9781680795875 (ebook) | ISBN 9781680796544 (Read-to-me ebook)

Subjects: LCSH: English language--Alphabet--Juvenile literature. | Alphabet
    books--Juvenile literature.

Classification: DDC 421/.1--dc23

LC record available at http://lccn.loc.gov/2016943880

Table of Contents

Aa 4

More Aa Words . . . 22

Glossary 23

Index 24

Abdo Kids Code . . . 24

Aa

Abby h**a**s fun with **a**unt **A**my.

Aa

Ad**a**m **a**cts silly in the b**a**th.

Aa

Ann**a a**sks if **A**be is **a**lright.

Aa

Ava looks for **a**nts.

Aa

Aiden thinks **a**lpacas **a**re **a**wesome.

Aa

Alex h**a**nd p**a**ints his **a**rt.

Aa

Avery c**a**n **add.**

16

8 + 3 = 11
10 + 5 = 15
6 + 7 = 13
10 + 8 = 18
4 + 5 = 1

17

Aa

Andy h**as an a**nswer.

Aa

What does **A**ndre**a** h**a**ve?

(**a**pples)

More Aa Words

accordion

alligator

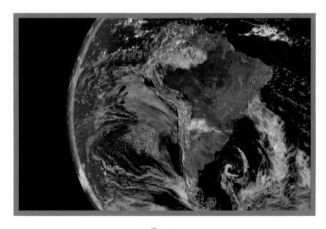
Africa

antlers

Glossary

add
put together two or more numbers to find their total value.

alpaca
a long-haired South American mammal.

Index

add 16

alpaca 12

answer 18

ant 10

apple 20

art 14

ask 8

aunt 4

bath 6

fun 4

paint 14

abdokids.com

Use this code to log on to abdokids.com and access crafts, games, videos, and more!